Healing in the Presence of the Lord
Devotional

Healing in the Presence of the Lord Devotional

Copyright (c) 2019 by Natalie Degraffinreaidt

All rights reserved. No part of this book may be reproduced or transmitted in any form or by any means without written permission of the author.

ISBN 978-1-947741-47-8

Book published by

        Kingdom Publishing LLC
        Odenton, MD 21113

        First printed in the U.S.A.

Dedication

This book is dedicated to my father above for His grace! I thank Him for His unfailing love that He has poured upon my life! This book is designed to devote my time back to my father! I can't thank Him enough for saving me from a burning hell! All I can do is honor Him by lifting His name up on high daily! I am forever grateful for the life God has provided for me. He has provided a way out of no way! He made a way of an escape for me and brought healing to my whole household! I thank God for His marvelous works that He has done in me! I honor Him through this book and pray someone else will receive hope, deliverance, guidance, healing and restoration. Be revived and be blessed from this book! Blessings and Peace unto each reader!

Table of Contents

Introduction 5

Chapter 1   Breaking Free 6

Chapter 2   Freedom 8

Chapter 3   Faith 10

Chapter 4   Trust 12

Chapter 5   Obedience 14

Chapter 6   Accepting the Call 16

Chapter 7   Walking into the Call 18

Chapter 8   New Beginning 20

Chapter 9   Restoration 22

Chapter 10   In Closing 24

About the Author 26

INTRODUCTION

This devotional is written for people to walk with me through my own healing process. This journey has been a long fight for my freedom, but I thank God for seeing fit to set me free; For who the Son sets free is free indeed! God could have left me in a burning hell, but he didn't! My goal is to help as many people possible as they journey with me through my own healing process! I know for myself that God is a healer! It's time to be healed in every area of your life, whether its mentally, physically, emotionally, sexually or spiritually!

God will heal every one of your open wounds by His divine power! He'll be your helper in the time of trouble! He'll shine light on every dark area in your life! As God takes you through your own healing experience…accept it, rejoice and move forward with your life! Don't stay stuck in your current condition but instead begin walking forward! Take baby steps into your healing!

If you have not already purchased my book or workbook it is definitely recommended. It will help you get a better feel for my process of healing and take you deeper into your own healing process! I'm excited you have decided to take this trying yet rewarding journey with me!

BREAKING FREE

Many times in life people say they want to be free from bondage. You hear people complain constantly about the same things, but refuse to make adjustments in their life in order to move forward. I just refuse to be that person. In order to live a free life, I must examine myself daily. Believe me, the truth is never easy to accept, but it's a must if you want to become free within yourself and live your best life ever!

Today, I'm reflecting on the things that I allowed to hold me back! I'm thinking about the power I gave away to other people who hurt me. I'm thinking about the time I lost trying to do things that were beneficial for other people and not for myself. I'm thinking about how I allowed abuse to define me. I'm thinking about the steps I am finally taking to get my life back on track! It's not easy, but it's necessary.

Below is a letter I wrote to myself:

Letter to self!

Self,

Thank you for finally taking a stand for yourself! You have always done things that were beneficial for other people! I am proud of you for finally making decisions best for you and your family! It took you a while, but you finally got it! You should be proud of yourself.

Now remember, this is just the beginning! You have a lot of catching up to do, but at least you are making progress by taking the proper steps necessary to reach your destiny. Give yourself credit for the things you have accomplished already and give honor to God daily for saving you from a burning hell! Now let's get working. Before you go think about how far you have come! Think about the beautiful person you are inside and out! Think about the blessings you have and remember to appreciate them daily! You were your biggest hindrance, but now you have decided to move yourself out of the way. I give you honor for submitting to the will of the father and not submitting to man's will and plan for your life! All along you have been the change you've been waiting on! Now that you know, you will be unstoppable! Have a wonderful day!

Signed by,

The New Version of You!

FREEDOM

There is a cost for your freedom. I am sitting here thanking God for freeing me from my past and present pain! The pain ran so deep within, it cost me my glow; I lost my true identity in Christ. The contamination of wrong things on this journey called life caused me repeat the same cycles over and over again.

In order for a change to come, I had to seek God daily and cry out to Him for my own deliverance! I went knocking at his door, asking Him to heal my brokenness. I was exposed before Him. God seen for who I was through His eyes and not the way people perceived me! He began cleaning me up and showing me my identity in Him!

The more the Lord revealed Himself to me, the more free I became in Him! The way other people perceived me no longer mattered. The love of God strengthened me in all of my weakness and reigned in my life.

This is the kind of love that is unexplainable, but it brings true freedom to your life! Everything that is not like Him will burn up before His sight!

I thank God for giving me freedom in Him because outside of Him is a life of hell and torment! In Him there is freedom and liberty! This fight is well worth it! The cost of this oil! Now, I walk more and more in my freedom that has been given to me in Christ. I'm not saying it's easy, but it is worth the fight! At the end your reward will be great!

PRAYER

Lord today, I come before your face to ask you to continually reveal my faults! Help me to walk upright daily before your face! Lead me to the places you want me to go! Help me to continuously be obedient to your will even when it doesn't feel good or I don't understand it! Thank you for imputing your righteousness into my life! Thank you for strengthening me in my weaknesses! Thank you for choosing me to live in you! You could have chosen anyone, but you chose me! I am forever grateful for your unfailing love. In Christ Jesus name, Amen!

FAITH

Faith, Faith, Faith!! Who can honestly say they have genuine faith in God's plan for their life?! I mean let's be real about it; God tells you to do something, but your natural eyes and intellect can't even fathom the instructions He gives. The reason why it can't be understood is because it doesn't seem obtainable or possible!

Believe me, I understand the feeling, but the word of God states that faith without works is dead. We can't expect God to move on our behalf if we don't take the first step of faith. In other words, if God tells you to forgive someone, reach out to someone, start your business idea, write your book, go for that promotion, etc.; you must have enough faith to follow His instructions and believe the word that was spoken to you.

On my journey, God constantly told me to do things that didn't make sense to me! I hesitated every time God told me to do something, but I also knew following His blue-print for my life was important. Today, I'm thinking about how God asked me to walk away from my job in order for me to obtain the abundant life in Him. My first thought was, not again Lord! How am I supposed to provide for my family? How am I going to reach the abundant life without having resources to put into my business? I felt a little discouraged not knowing how things were going to work out in my favor.

I began crying out to God, reminding Him of what He told me; to walk away from these things in order to obtain the abundant life! You told me you were going to bless me exponentially! You told me Oh God to start this Radio/T.V. Show, but I don't even have the resources to sustain the work! What am I supposed to do now?

That was my heart cry to God today! His response to me was simple. It's by my power and strength not by yours! Your family and the people around you will see that I am with you! The people around you will call you blessed. Keep walking right into your blessings! Keep moving forward! I'm with you to carry you through. Faith is the substance of things hoped for, the evidence of things not seen.

I straightened myself up quick and said okay God! I have enough faith to trust what you are speaking to me! When God speaks, His word will accomplish what it was sent out to do.

I'm closing with this; have enough faith to believe God for your promise! Remember, without faith it is impossible to please God! All you need is faith as small as a mustard seed. Exercise your faith and watch it grow!

PRAYER

Father God, I pray you help increase my faith every day! I know that I cannot do anything without faith! Your word says, "Faith without works is dead"! Help me begin working out my faith in the areas you speak to me. Allow me to be moved out of the way and to believe your word for my life! Allow me to trust your blue-print for my life and not people's blue-print for my life! Thank you for choosing me to take this faith journey in you! In Christ Jesus Name, Amen!

TRUST

I have experienced a lot of trauma throughout my journey in life, so trust is a major factor for me. I had a major issue trusting people with my heart. I finally let my guard down to trust people and my heart was damaged again. I grew cold. I didn't want to be bothered with individuals any longer and unforgiveness festered in my spirit.

I had to ask God to clean those wounds up and help me to forgive the people who hurt me. I had to learn that God forgives me daily, so who am I to not forgive other people? Where much is given, much is required! I'm not saying it was easy, but it's a must in order to live a healthy life in Christ!

I had to re-open myself up to these individuals. Could you imagine how I felt when God revealed that I was connected to certain people in order to carry out His plan! Believe me it was a hard pill to swallow, but I knew trusting God was a must. He's been teaching me through this whole process how to trust him in spite of what I see. He also revealed to me; who am I to not open myself back up to these people? What if he didn't re-open himself up to me every time I trespassed against him?

I must count the cost for my anointing and trust my process, but must importantly trust God with my life! I've already made a mess of my life and it's time for me to surrender to the source that is greater than I. The abundant life will then be attracted to me! My choice is to trust God's plan for my life.

PRAYER

Lord, I trust you with my life! I know it's a struggle with me at times, but I know you will never leave me nor forsake me. God help me to re-open myself up to the people who have deeply wounded me. Help me to trust people again; help me to continue trusting your plan for my life. Your word states in Proverbs, "Trust the Lord with all thine heart and lean not on your own understanding…" Help me to lean on You in all my ways and not on myself! My heart's desire is to fulfill your purpose for me in this earth. Thank you for rescuing me from myself! I will continue to trust your plan! Father, I realize the depth of my pain comes from the amount of love stored up in my heart for these individuals. My love for them is pure and uncontaminated, but I know they are on their own journey as well. I will forgive them and continue to love them. Please help me step by step to trust them with my heart again. The pain I experienced caused me major setbacks in my life, but I can't afford any more setbacks father! In all my ways and actions, I look to you! In Christ Jesus Name, Amen!

OBEDIENCE

How many people know, obedience is better than sacrifice? I mean really, obedience is better than sacrifice! This is mentioned all throughout the bible! The thing you are trying to sacrifice to God; just may not be what He requires from you! For example, God could tell you to reach out to someone, but instead, you say God, I would rather pray for the individual. You praying for the individual isn't what God required from you! God required for you to reach out to the individual. Obedience is better than sacrifice! You never know the reason God instructs you to contact a person.

Our job is to be obedient to his commands. Your phone call could stop the person from committing suicide, it could brighten their day, or the person could be a blessing to you! Don't miss your own blessings because of your disobedience. God calls for us to be obedient to Him by following His instructions.

Believe me, I'm stubborn and I struggle with obedience. It's not something I am proud of because my own stubbornness is what has prevented me from carrying out certain tasks God gave to me. In other words, it delayed the process. I didn't want to carry out the assignment because of the people that were attached to the assignment. Believe me when I tell you, God will win! Every fiber in your body will be broken down, until your obedience is complete in Him. Take it from me, I'm a living witness! Through my struggle, I still choose obedience so that God's will can be done in my life.

PRAYER

Lord, please help me be obedient to your will for my life! Help me to follow your commands and not sacrifice your will for my life, due to my own stubbornness. Help me continuously be open to change, so your will for my life can manifest itself. Please bring forth any thoughts in my mind that could cause me to not be obedient to your will. Help me take those thoughts captive, so my obedience will become complete in you. In Christ Jesus Name, Amen!

ACCEPTING THE CALL

Accepting the call! Who can handle the cost of the call?!?! This is a call that will cost you much. Everything you thought you had gained will be lost in order for you to find your life in Christ. Let's think for a moment; imagine your earthly parents calling your phone, but you don't answer. I don't know about anyone else's parents, but my mother will keep calling me until I pick up that phone and answer her.

Even though she's doing her part by calling me, it is my choice to answer the call or not. Many times, if my mom calls me while I'm in the middle of doing something, instead of answering the call, I'll continue to let the phone ring. The phone will ring over and over and over again, but I will act as if I don't hear it. I don't want to stop in the middle of what I'm doing to answer the call.

This is exactly how it is when God calls us! He will keep calling and calling, but it's up to us to answer the call. The word states that many are called, but few are chosen. Everyone won't answer the call, in fact many people will reject the call. Personally, I didn't feel as though I had any other choice but to accept the call of God for my life. Accepting this call was very painful but forever changing.

Today, in my quiet time with the Lord, He gave me another set of instructions. Once the instructions were given to me, I took some time to digest and process what He was saying to me. I had to let go of everything that didn't serve me any purpose or didn't align with His calling for my life. I had to walk away from my job! I had to walk away from the political campaign that I was managing. I was pulled away from everything I believed was for me until God intervened to show me his blueprint for my life. This was such a hard pill to swallow! I didn't know how my bills were going to get paid or how my business was going to survive without any resources.

God let me know that he is in control and I must obey Him. He is leading me to the land to possess it. He will sustain me, but I must accept the call and walk into it. Accepting the call was still hard, but I had to do it! When God calls you, He will disrupt everything in your life. My advice to everyone is to accept the call from God for your life. It won't feel good, but its working for your good! He is the alpha and the omega! He knows your end from your beginning!

PRAYER

Father God, please help me to accept what you are doing in my life. Allow me to understand the importance of carrying out your plan for my life. Give me the strength to release anything that's not pleasing to you or in alignment with your call for my life. I thank you for choosing me! In Christ Jesus Name, Amen!

WALKING INTO THE CALLING

Now this was so hard for me! This was an ongoing process where I had to forget about everything I thought I knew and accept the revelations God had given to me. I had to forgive constantly and release people from the pain they afflicted upon me. Holding these people hostage in my spirit only hindered my calling. I took every experience as a learning experience and turned it into something positive.

Today, I'm meditating on the people God had to remove from my life. He removed them for my own growth so that I could be grounded in Him. God needed me to seek Him for answers and not allow people to define my calling in Him. He wanted to let me know that He already validated my call. My call didn't come from man, but from Him! It was up to me to accept it and walk into the things He was calling me to do!

I had such a hard time walking into the call He had for my life. It was difficult because of the love that I carried for the people that He removed from my life. It was hard to accept that these people were not healthy for me. It was hard accepting that these people were only feeding my negative emotions. I was allowing my own insecurities and lack of faith to emotionally attach myself to situations, which was only killing the real me. I finally made a conscious decision to walk into my calling.

PRAYER

Father God, please help me to continue moving forward into the calling on my life. Allow my eyes to stay fixed on you! Father God please help me to be the woman you called me to be in you! Thank you for allowing me to see the damage that being emotionally attached to people will cause. Thank you for helping heal my heart by removing these relationships and most importantly thank you for helping me to accept this process in my life. Please help me to continue to forgive daily! I don't know what I would do without you oh God, but in you I have found safety. Thank you for loving me so much! In Christ Jesus Name, Amen!!

NEW BEGINNING

In order for something to become new, you must be willing to let go of the old and get rid of it. Have you ever seen a hoarder? A hoarder is someone who accumulates things over time. When it's time for them to let these items go, they find reasons to preserve them for a cause. The items the hoarder is holding on to is taking up space where the new things should be.

Instead of getting rid of the old the hoarder will continue to mix the new items in the same space with the old. What a bad combination! Have you ever been in someone's house that hoards everything? It can make you quite uncomfortable!

When God calls us to the new, it will make us quite uncomfortable! Every negative habit or negative cycle of behavior will be brought to your attention! God will demand a change in your behavior in order to obtain the new!

I know for me, I had to release every negative emotion and deal with every negative cycle. I had to begin washing myself with the word of God, which brought a renewing of my mind! I had to change the way I viewed things with my own human intellect. I had to see things with the eyes of Christ. I had to continue digging for the root of the issue, in order to be properly healed from it.

The more I poured out the old and released it to God, I was able to receive the new! God was able to fill me up with His spirit as I surrendered my negative thought patterns, my old habits and my pain to Him! Once God filled me up with His spirit, He empowered me to see things in a different light. He changed my mindset and opened the eyes of my understanding to more of His word. He brought a sense of inner peace upon my life. He helped me begin to make the necessary steps in my life to climb out of my present circumstances. He brought clarity to my life and helped me to take better care of myself first.

This is new for me! I am so used to taking care of everyone else. My whole life I've looked out for others; did what was best for others and never invested in myself! I have always put other people's feeling and happiness before my own. Now it is time to invest in me! Investing in myself is a part of my healing and to walk away from the past life. I am learning more and more to enjoy me!

PRAYER

Father God, please continue to allow me to empty out all negative emotions. My heart's desire is to do Your will. I don't want anything to fester in me that's not of you. Please father, continue to reveal my thoughts to me! Expose anything in me that's not of you! Continue to shine your light in any dark areas in my life. Help me to make the necessary changes, in order to walk in the new! Thank you for giving me another chance at life! Thank you for healing me continuously from the affliction of others. Thank you for allowing me to learn more about myself and my purpose in You! In You is where I found my being! Thank you for filling me up with your power! In Christ Jesus Name, Amen!!

RESTORATION

Restoration, Restoration!! How many people understand that something broken, cannot fix something broken? Better yet, something damaged is not fixed for use. How can something possibly broken fix anything? If you buy a box of drinking glasses and open the box to see the glasses are damaged, what good are they? You can't make use of the broken glasses and will need to return the damaged items.

I hope you were able to understand the above metaphors. Now let's talk about my life for a moment. I'm thinking about how damaged I was still trying to help other people. I found it quite amusing how even though I was a damaged good, my intentions were to fix other damaged goods. I was a natural born fixer, but the only problem is something that's damaged is useless until it is returned and put back to together to gain its proper value.

In this season of my life, God is restoring me back to my proper place in Him. He had to heal every open wound that caused me to be unfit for His use. God had to examine every part of my being so that ultimately, I could be sustained in Him! He had to reveal my true-identity inside of Him and not my identity inside of a building or from people. He had to restore my identity in order to continue on this journey in Him.

God had to break me free from people and myself so that I could seek out His purpose for my life. This has been a rewarding process for me. I've learned a lot about myself! I'm able to face myself, deal with myself, love myself, live with myself, accept myself, treat myself, appreciate myself and most importantly lean on God's guidance for my life! He is restoring everything back to me that I've lost over the years! He's bringing me to a place of true essence in Him. I seek God daily before making any decisions! I understand now the importance of self-discipline. I thank God for endowing me with His power to move forward into the unknown in Him!

Moving forward into the unknown is scary, but rewarding. He's teaching me how to trust in Him and not in myself! He's bringing my faith back to life! He's teaching me to believe in the dream He placed inside of me and to listen to His voice! He's teaching me to understand, I'm worthy of the call and the assignment He has placed upon my life! He's teaching me to remain still and know that He is God! He's teaching me the power of my words! He's allowing me to see the beauty of life. He restored me back into my right mind in Him! I am forever thankful for God's unfailing love! He has showed me that I am enough! He has taught me to know my value and to love on myself.

His presence has brought much revelation and closure to my life. I can't thank God enough for saving me from myself. His presence has brought true, divine healing to my life. If he did it for me, believe me he'll do it for you. God is not a respecter of persons. Just trust Him.

IN CLOSING

I hope this devotional blessed your life. I pray you take the time out to allow God to speak to you through this devotional. God is a healer and He is able to do the impossible! He will turn your mess around for His glory. All you need to do is trust Him and knock at His door for guidance. Knock and the door will be open to you.

He will invite you in to show you things about yourself, so that you can receive your healing. He'll clean you up, mold you, shape you and send you forth for His use. I ask you to embrace this process. I'm not saying it's easy; it will be painful before it's rewarding, but it's worth it.

I'm grateful God took me through this process. It's making me a better version of myself. I'm definitely not the same person. I see things in a different light and understand God for who He really is for myself. Not through mere man, heresays or any other form of intellect, but I know Him for myself!

Getting to know God for yourself is vital. You can get to know Him by seeking Him with an open heart and with the right intentions. Be prepared to repent from your old ways and the weaker elements of this world, so that you can enter His Kingdom.

I had to call out every sin one by one and ask God for His forgiveness. I had to repent of every sin that came to my conscious mind. It had to be a genuine repentance of remorse for trespassing against God. I cried out and studied these sins one by one. I carefully observed them to correct the errors of my ways and prevent these errors from reoccurring in my bloodline.

I thank everyone for your support and pray blessings upon your life! May God fill you up with His spirit... as He empties out everything that's not of Him. Be of good courage and trust God through your own healing process! If you haven't purchased the "Healing in The Presence of The Lord" book or workbook, I strongly encourage you to purchase it. These books will allow you to follow along with me on my journey! Walk with me as I walk into my new fulfilling life in Christ.

Blessings to each reader,

The New Version of Natalie In Christ

NATALIE DEGRAFFINREAIDT
About the Author

Natalie is a devoted wife to Warren Degraffinreaidt and mother of four wonderful children, Ariannah, Quincy, Warren III and Terrell. She is not only an author, but a playwriter and dancer. She is devoted to serving the community and is a warrior for the lost.

Natalie gave her life to Christ and is a woman after God's own heart. Her lifelong journey is warring for souls. She believes that through praying and fasting, and being led by the Spirit of Christ, she can tell her story in love and truth and bring many people to Christ.

Natalie has created a nonprofit organization, Blossoming Seeds, which is solely for people who have been mentally, verbally, sexually, emotionally, physically abused, along with those who has succomb to the abuse of drugs and alcohol. She has created programs to meet the needs of people who have suffered from such trauma.

1 Corinthians 3:6
"I planted the seed, Apollo watered the plant...but it was God who made the plant to grow."

www.ingramcontent.com/pod-product-compliance
Lightning Source LLC
Chambersburg PA
CBHW052210110526
44591CB00012B/2162